Mercury HeartLink

DITCHBANK DIARIES

Haibuñera from

the Land of Enchantment

SHIRLEY BALANCE BLACKWELL

Ditchbank Diaries: *Haibuñera from the Land of Enchantment*
Copyright ©2013 Shirley Balance Blackwell
ISBN: 978-0-9892882-3-1
Publisher: Mercury HeartLink
Printed in the United States of America

Interior images by Louis Blackwell.
Back cover portrait and frontispiece by Georgia Santa-Maria.
Front cover photograph "Alcalde Ditch" by Stewart S. Warren.

Contact the author: *www.shirleyblackwell.com*

Mercury HeartLink
www.heartlink.com

Contents

Foreword by
José A. Rivera, Ph.D.   *XI*

Introduction   *XV*

Author's Note   *XVII*

Dedication   *XIX*

I.

ANCIENTS AND ANCESTORS

ACEQUIA MADRE   3
TWO SONGS TO THE MOTHER   5

A LONG LINEAGE   7
LET US SHARE   9

PRAYER IN A TIME OF DROUGHT   11
RAIN DANCE   13

CELL PHONE CABALLERO   15
SAFE PASSAGE   17

II.
What Counts

Measuring What Matters   *21*

Monsoon   *23*

Bosque del Apache   *25*

Legacy   *27*

III.
Nature's Purest Ray,
Sharpest Claw

Oasis and Fortress   *31*

Sanctuary   *33*

Hunting Grounds   *35*

Cuatro   *37*

Of Bird Counts and Counterfeiters   *39*

Repository   *41*

Paseo de las Floridas   *43*

Bouquet Olé   *45*

IV.
SACRED LAND, SACRED WATER

LAS CONCHAS FIRE   49
NOVENA DE LAS LÁGRIMAS   51

SAN YSIDRO LABRADOR   53
FRAY JUAN CHACÓN BLESSES THE NEW DITCH   55

V.
LA COMUNA

MAYORDOMO   59
DITCH RIDER   61

AUXILIO   63
QASIDA OF FAITH   65

SACAR LA ACEQUIA   67
DÍA DE LA SACA   69

POLITICAL CURRENTS   71
WATER DEMOCRACY   73

VI.
FOLKLÓRICO

LA LLORONA, THE WEEPING WOMAN   77
CROSSROADS ACROSTIC   79

FISH AND GAME DEPARTMENT   81
SILENT PARTNER   83

EVERY DAY A FEAST DAY   85
COMIDA REAL   87

VII.
HEALING WATERS

CANINE ENCOUNTERS   91
BUT I WILL GRIEVE FOR YOU   93

COVERING HIS TRACKS   95
VARIATIONS ON KID ORY'S TUNE   97

MEASURING THE FLOW   99
HIGH EXPECTATIONS   101

EPHEMERA OF CONSEQUENCE   103
WHY I DON'T WRITE YOU LOVE POEMS   105

UNBRIDLED CONFIDENCE   107
JUST A LINE TO SAY . . .   109

Acknowledgments   111

About the Author   115

Foreword by
José A. Rivera, Ph.D.

A professor in the School of Architecture and Planning at the University of New Mexico (UNM), Prof. Rivera is also a research scholar at UNM's Center for Regional Studies. His peers regard him as the preeminent authority on acequia culture of the upper Rio Grande.

When I wrote *Acequia Culture* in 1998, little did I know that more than a dozen years later the subject matter of the book would attract the attention of a masterful poet, Shirley Blackwell. Her published work in *Already There* (2011) set up a methodology that fits her inquisitive nature: combine investigative rigor with the freedom to speak from the heart by exploring the impact of the cosmos on the human spirit.

For this present volume, Blackwell was inspired by the network of roads that sit atop the ancient earthen canals of rural New Mexico known as *acequias*, a simulacra of Medieval Iberian irrigation communities. Her objective was to recover the stories of life as told by "the denizens of the ditchbanks" whether as wildlife, domesticated species, or the human *vecinos*, neighbors. Each of these living creatures depends on water as the vital fluid that creates and sustains life, knowledge that we proclaim in bumper sticker media as, "*el agua es vida,* water is life."

In Spanish, the ditchbank is often expressed as the *bordo*, a path for walking along an irrigation canal that in design also sets the boundary for community as place. Of necessity, its line follows the natural contours of the land, a function of gravity-flow irrigation that is carbon free and does not mine the groundwater aquifers. These ditches create greenways in the ribbons of irrigated fields, acting much like sponges that retain water, control soil erosion, recharge the aquifers, nurture the cottonwood bosques and other native vegetation, and shelter fish and wildlife habitats in the shaded space of the acequia microclimate.

Nestled within the canyons and valley floors, acequia-based villages still dot the uplands of the Rio Grande, where earthen engineering works—the acequias—divert water to extend life into every tract and pocket of arable bottomland. In each place, the acequia watercourse is the most distinguishing feature of the community and its relationship to the surrounding open and rural landscape: the watercourse shapes the edges of the varied terrain; defines natural and human-made boundaries, sets limits to growth; allocates space for community development and the built environment; and nourishes plant and animal ecology within the corridor.

In the acequia *imaginary*—that archetype, concept, or mythological construct humans attach to a place or way of life—connections with the geography are an integral part of individual as well as collective identity. Everyone is "from a place," but place encompasses more than physical location.

Blackwell lives in the middle stretch of the Rio Grande Valley, in the vicinity of Los Lunas, a village south of Albuquerque that also had roots as a Spanish water colony. Although not born into or raised in the acequia culture of the Rio Grande, she grew up in desert country and has now lived in this rural village for some sixteen years. By now, and as evidenced by the insightful prose essays and poems within the seven chapters of *Ditchbank Diaries*, she has shed her "newcomer" identity and has blended with the denizens who live along the *bordo*.

This ditchbank is what weds all the neighbors into a commons, a parallel universe that Blackwell as poet "discovered" a few years after her return to her home state. Her fascination for the wildlife and natural world supported by the local acequia evolved into intriguing explorations of the *bordo*, where the footpath along the ditch put her into a direct connection with the acequia dwellers and their life stories. That connection is what brought Blackwell to explore this new world and pen her diaries with factual information alongside memorable images, using a novel invention juxtaposing prose essays with paired poems, all the while adhering to a discipline of self-imposed rules. Her prose and poetry in this volume describe the *acequia madre* and its baby ditches, the bosque of wildlife, the complexity of the sacred land along with the rituals and folklore of *la comuna*, the nine days of the Conchas on fire, the wailing of *La Llorona* as she walks the ditchbank at night, and fittingly, she ends with a number of compositions about healing waters.

As expected, we find prose and poetry about the iconic *mayordomo*, the recurring *limpia* or *día de la saca* when ditches are cleaned out to start the irrigation season, along with the blessing of the fields on the feast day of the patron saint, San Ysidro, and other commonly known events that occur on or in proximity to the ditchbank.

In addition, and to her credit, Blackwell also incorporates subject matter known mostly to specialists. Her investigative bent, a desire to enrich her material with historical context, prompted her to research and then include details about the medieval officer of Spanish irrigation, the *cequier*; the intricacies of water sharing among acequia irrigators, such as the concept of *auxilio*; colonial laws about land and water expressed in the Spanish *ordenanzas*; and other nuances of acequia antiquity that persist to this day. Likely, the inclusion of these and other historical intricacies will prompt readers to delve into acequia research of their own.

In the end, Blackwell succeeds in meeting her goal: the notes from her diaries let you share a stroll into a parallel universe inhabited by denizens of the acequia imaginary. Throughout her journey, the ditchbank is her—and our—point of view. This approach is novel and leads readers in with curiosity and anticipation of what will come in the next pairing of informative prose with thought-provoking poem. Once you start down her ditchbank path, you will find it difficult to stop or step aside.

—José A. Rivera, Albuquerque, NM, April 2013

INTRODUCTION

A favorite plot line in science fiction literature is one in which the protagonist steps into a parallel universe that has hitherto been invisible or unsuspected in the hero's home world. When I began taking daily walks along the acequias (ah-SEK-ias) of New Mexico's middle Rio Grande, I discovered myself in such a universe.

At first, I was fascinated by the richness of wildlife and natural beauty that acequias supported just outside my door. Next, I became intrigued by the complex network of roads atop the ditchbanks, a system that interlaces our rural community. These roads provide travel routes that extend miles on end for foot, horse, or even some motorized traffic; for years I had barely noticed they were there.

Gradually, I got to know denizens of the ditchbanks—wild, domesticated, and human—and began to uncover stories of life in an acequia community. It is hard to overstate the importance of acequia societies in New Mexico's environment, history, culture, and identity. Especially for residents of the upper Rio Grande (Rio Arriba) and to a lesser degree, those living in the middle and lower river (Rio Abajo), acequias represent more than a technology. They embody a way of life and a moral compass.

What little has been written about acequia culture deals mostly with water laws, anthropological studies, hydrology, and other scholarly research that demands objectivity. A few visual artists and musicians have made acequias their subject. I am grateful that, with poetry, I also have the freedom to explore, subjectively, the impact that this parallel universe can have on the individual spirit.

Author's Note

This work experiments with a new poetry form inspired by Japanese haibun. I was intrigued by the concept of pairing a lyrical and image-rich prose essay/diary entry/travelogue with a highly structured small poem. I knew from the outset that the haibun's "snapshot in time" would not provide adequate scope for this project's subject matter of acequia ecology, tradition, and culture in New Mexico, the Land of Enchantment. Still, I relished the challenge of working in a confined space; so, I set simple rules:

> Each poem pair consists of an introductory prose piece, which may be prose poem, vignette, or expository essay; it cannot exceed 300 words, excluding the title and any translations or explanations of terms. The prose piece will be partnered by a form poem, which shall contain 12 lines or have 12 components; these may include the title.

> The small, companion poem, like the haiku of traditional haibun, may relate directly to the prose or simply be suggested by it. Unlike the haiku of haibun, the companion poem will have its own title.

I chose 300 words because I wanted to convey information, as well as impressions. I chose 12 lines or components (single words, groups of words, syllables, metrical feet, etc.) because that number offered many potential configurations for rhyme or meter and enough room to tell a story.

A self-imposed task was to use as many variations in pattern as I could, especially those relating to my theme of acequias, which derived from pre-15th Century Islamic Spain. Included in this work is a poem containing two variations of the Spanish sextilla. I also wrote a qasida and a ghazal, in homage to the Arabic underpinnings of acequia societies. I improvised on a recent invention, the Fibonacci poem, because the Fibonacci sequence on which it is based was developed by Arab mathematicians.

I have named my invention *haibuñera*. The combination of *haibun* with the word *habañera* was at first just an amusing exercise in punning, but it began to seem more appropriate as I researched the interchange of Old and New World cultures associated with Spanish exploration of the Americas. I learned that Spanish sailors took the *habañera*, a cyclic Cuban dance, back to those regions of Islamic Spain (Andalucia, Valencia, and Alicante) where acequia culture originated, and *habañera*, in turn, became part of Spain's popular culture.

I was also gratified to find that the *habañera* was the first contra-dance to which lyrics were sung. In my *haibuñera*, I aspire to enliven a prescribed pattern of steps with music and a dance of words.

DEDICATION

This book is dedicated to the only possible choice: ditchbank companion, life companion, soul's companion, father of our children, fiddler of merit, and true love for nearly fifty years—my husband, Louis Blackwell. Even at this stage in our lives, you have made me fall in love all over again, or was it just the magic of our walks along the ditchbanks?

DITCHBANK DIARIES

I.

ANCIENTS AND ANCESTORS

ACEQUIA MADRE

As the snowcaps on rugged peaks of the lower Rockies melt in New Mexico's vernal sun, rivulets begin a journey down their destined side of a great demarcation, the Continental Divide. The shining trickles grow to rivers and thread the desert floor on pilgrimage to the Pacific Ocean or the Gulf of Mexico. Woven into the riverbanks, forest borders called *bosque* (BOHS-keh) promenade willow, cottonwood, and plum. These sinuous oases support life of myriad forms amid unforgiving terrain of arid soils and infrequent rain. But it is water–agua–around which all else revolves: survival, community, culture, wealth, and law.

Indigenous pueblo people once plied tree-snag plows and wooden hoes to harvest life-giving flows of Rio Chama, Rio Grande, and Rio Pecos for sun-drenched fields of blue corn, beans, and squash. Twelve centuries later, vestiges of their work remain: the natives' stone-lined canals have been upgraded and renamed in lilting Spanish phrases, but their function stays the same. Hispanic colonists called them *acequias*, and that term lives on; but in the modern parlance of New Mexicans, *ditches* is the name by which they are known.

"Mother" ditches feeding "baby" ditches are known as *acequias madres*, and they thread this mystic land that is so deeply imbued with veneration of the feminine; where, to this day, women plant a child's umbilicus beneath stream-fed tree or bush to seal the baby's bond with Mother Earth; where Changing Woman brought forth the Hero Twins to help the Dinè vanquish Cloud Swallower, a monster who drank the heavens dry; where, on a shaded plaza, the visage of La Virgen de Guadalupe, carved into a century-old cottonwood, turns toward a fountain gurgling below a chiseled stone cross.

Notes for the companion poem:

In the Tiwa language, there are no personal pronouns. A woman such as Naotsete would speak of herself as "a woman." Her entire song is what she would have spoken aloud.

Tse-pi'na translates as "Woman Veiled in Clouds," known today as Mt. Taylor

Since 1531, when a peasant reported seeing her image surrounded by light near Mexico City, La Virgen de Guadalupe has become the most popular religious and cultural icon for Hispanics in the New World.

El cequier (SEK-ee-yer) was the overseer chosen by la comuna (community of irrigators) to regulate distribution of water. This very early term would have been used by a woman of Consuelo's era and meant the same as today's *mayordomo*, or *ditch boss*.

Two Songs to the Mother

I. Naotsete's Offering

Beneath a juniper, A Woman plants the cord
of birth to bind to Mother Earth a newborn son.
Tse-pi'na! Hear the water song that flows in dry-seed gourd.
Delight in raindrop dance of fingers on the deerhide drum.
Where tassels float in prayer over hills of young blue corn,
release refreshing waters to waken sacred loam.

II. Consuelo's Prayer

¡Virgen de Guadalupe! This Baca widow kneels. My womb
has borne no sons to tend my late husband's fields, yet my toil
finds its defender in the courts of Spanish custom.
El cequier deals honorably; I will receive my dole.
I am shielded from the greed of my neighbor, Mondragón.
A candle for you, Lady. Agua flows to Baca soil!

A Long Lineage

Ditch irrigation is as old as the ancient kingdoms of Egypt, Babylonia, and Persia. By the Iron Age, aqueducts called *falaj* watered fields in Oman and filled royal baths in India. A limestone conduit 50 miles long supplied water to the Assyrian capital of Ninevah seven centuries BCE. Imperial Roman engineers perfected and named their marvels *aqueducts*, from the Latin *aqua* (water) and *ducere* (to lead).

Near Nazca, Peru, aqueducts called *puquios*, built in the 6th Century CE, are still in use. The Aztec capital, Tenochtitlán, had working aqueducts when the first Spanish arrived in the early 1500s.

The differences between aqueducts and acequias are more fundamental than might first be apparent. Aqueducts separate water from the land; acequias integrate it with the land. *Aqueduct* connotes function, *acequia* invokes feeling.

The word *acequia* derives from the Arabic *as-sāqiya*, which means both "water conduit" and the poetically nuanced "cupbearer." Arabs brought acequia technology to the Spanish provinces of Valencia and Andalucia while occupying the Iberian Peninsula during 711-1492 CE. These *Musulmanes*, as they were called in Spanish, also introduced norms of communal behavior that have sustained irrigation communities worldwide throughout history.

As the Spanish pushed north from Mexico, they found indigenous water systems that must have seemed eerily familiar and which, in some areas, dated back for centuries. Ironically, as principles of acequia community adopted from Spain's conquerors were codified into law, they gave some protection to those irrigation societies the Spanish sought to conquer in the Americas. King Philip II of Castille had decreed* that Hispanic colonists in the New World must respect indigenous water rights—even as they stripped Native Americans of other human rights.

Scholars* consider traditional acequia communities to be cultural treasures. New Mexico and Colorado have enacted laws recognizing acequias' contribution to the common good.

*King Philip II of Spain established clear guidelines for Spanish colonization in the New World in his *Ordenanzas de Descubrimiento, Nueva Población de las Indias dadas por Felipe II en 1573* (*Laws of the Indies*). The rules forbade colonists to usurp water supplies being used by indigenous peoples or to overburden the colonies' own resources. Overpopulated Spanish settlements sometimes had to split off or relocate.

**Noticias de las Acequias*, July 2012, citing Dr. Manuel Montoya's address, "Finding Global Heritage in Indigenous Agricultural Land Usage" at 5th Annual *Celebrando las Acequias*, June 2012.

LET US SHARE

A limestone flume streams liquid life to share
In Nineveh, Beloved, let us share!

No beauty bursts from sealed off aqueducts.
My Lord, our neighbors thirst. "No drop to share."

Ramona scents acequias running full.
Perfume of raindrops adds to fragrance shared.

A trickle is a kiss for aquifer.
Rapscallion ditch, your Fate we humans share!

A muskrat swims beneath acequia's reeds,
Stalks tremble when nose skims to breathe his share.

Sweet Poet, with your pen and ink declare,
Our Mother Earth will bless us, if we share!

PRAYER IN A TIME OF DROUGHT

We set out early this hot morning to beat the searing heat. Record highs for days on end, and unprecedented wind. Our year already halfway around the sun, and only twelve hundreths inch of rain, under three inches since last June.

The sky is a blistering sapphire hue above the Manzano Range, a draperied horizon swathed in lavender and powder blue. There, behind the rim, a horsetail of vapor, but is it distant jet or just my distant dream? No matter; a single cloud, too high, too thin to offer any promise for today. July Fourth is coming soon; perhaps the fireworks will start this year's monsoon. I wish it to be true, this old wives' tale told me by my mother and believed by so many others in this desert—that celebratory bursts will trigger storms for which our parched land thirsts.

We are just the latest generation to send our supplications skyward:

as the ancients we call Anasazi* must have done,
and after them the Tiwa, with their hardened feet
stamping to the rhythms of hollowed, hide-strung drum,
and after them, colonos hispanos, clacking wooden beads,
imploring San Ysidro to bless their fields in a time of need,
and after them, the ranchers' wives, sloshing water in tin pails
from horse trough or meandering creek to veranda rails
laced with Spanish roses: yellow, coral-rouged, and red.

---

*Anasazi were ancestral puebloans who inhabited areas from Casas Grandes in Mexico to Mesa Verde in Colorado. In New Mexico, their most famous dwelling place was Chaco Canyon, which they occupied from at least 800 CE until about 1200 CE.

Rain Dance

Clouds
flirt,
pose; flounce
petticoats
of rain; play coquette

in swirling, ballroom skirts. In arms
of handsome mountains, shower charms.

Desert suitors fret,
cannot boast;
hopes trounced,
hurt,
proud.

CELL PHONE CABALLERO

Antonio Aragón says his family owned all this land 400 years ago. From Valencia Ditch, where we now stand, it stretched south beyond Tomé Hill, which lies four miles away. The west boundary was marked by that low ridge on the other side of the river. It is three miles from here to the Rio Grande, so we estimate the ridge at five or six. Succeeding generations have divided the homestead, Antonio says, but the viejos remember the big spread in its heyday. That much land could make a man feel like a king.

✧

As we walk briskly along the El Cerro Ditch road, the approaching figures grow larger in the slanting autumn light. In the lead, the ebony Arabian stallion glides a half-length ahead and two hands taller than the roan. The riders could be father and son. No question who commands, by presence if not word. The tall, patrician man sits high, his supple back rising straight from the cantle of his ornate Spanish saddle. Both he and his mount gleam with old wealth's subtle signs. Engraved leather studded with silver lies like a sculpture on the stallion's back. Cross-and-berry conchos richly burnished with age ring the crown of the man's flat-brimmed gaucho hat.

The fingers of his left hand curve lightly around slack reigns resting on the saddlehorn, as the horse maintains a steady pace. Whether they know this path by rote, commands are shared thoughts, or the merest pressure of a knee directs the proud equine, there is no sign of coercion; man and horse move as one. The rider lifts a slender cell phone. Beneath his Zorro mustache, Spanish phrases spill in rapid-fire profusion, leap in post-Castillean radio frequencies to the ears of waiting workers.

SAFE PASSAGE

Señor Elegante,
you ride your conquistador legacy
as if it were the stallion between your silver spurs.

Your generations of Aragóns,
Bacas, and Griegos have rechristened
with young saints' names the Elders' revered mountains;

made hunchbacked Kokopelli, curved over minstrel flute,
trade his sack of seeds for an alien, bent-back burden;
appropriated symbol, worship, dress, as if indigenous lore

were yours by virtue of Don Felipe's royal fiat.
Still, by the law of that same Castillean king: unless clearly
abandoned, Native waterworks remained—inviolate.

II.

WHAT COUNTS

MEASURING WHAT MATTERS

The Land of Enchantment is the fifth largest U.S. state. It embraces 121,666 square miles, of which 234 square miles, or .2 percent, is covered by water. The headwaters of the Rio Grande rise in southern Colorado, then head south toward the Gulf of Mexico, roughly bisecting New Mexico. Towns are strung like stone beads along the river's coppery chain, which runs about 400 miles through the state.

There is no spot in New Mexico where one cannot see a mountain on one of the state's 278 clear days a year. Dry, thin air, vast plains, and sunlit snowcaps make towering peaks visible at a distance. From Albuquerque's 10,678-foot Sandia Crest, one can see the Sangre de Cristo Mountains, at least 80 miles northeast. This range cradles the Santa Fe and Carson National Forests, whose watersheds swell the Rio Grande.

Although the largest, the Rio Grande is not the only river watering this high desert landscape. Rio Ruidoso, Rio Tularosa, and Rio Bonito originate in a 40-mile stretch of volcanic range called Sierra Blanca, named for its dazzling winter crown of snow. The Mescalero Apaches hold Sierra Blanca Peak sacred and control access to its summit, which lies within reservation borders. The 12,003-foot Peak dominates the landscape and can be seen from Sandia Crest by looking 140 miles southeast.

Water for drinking and agriculture in New Mexico comes from snowpack in alpine mountains, intermittent rains and scant snowfall on the plains, a few rivers (small by the standards of most Americans), reservoirs behind dams on those rivers, and a July-to-September monsoon season that pushes Albuquerque's average annual rainfall to 8.69 inches.

In this landscape, a surveyor would do well to add two instruments to his toolkit: imagination and humility.

MONSOON

Over mountain flanks and desert thighs,
nimbus shadows glide with cooling kisses,
arouse dry succulents and thin-blade grasses,
tease with tongues of promise, humid eyes.

First drops join with earth in rare perfume: their notes
of dust and dampness lie in shade, commingled.
Showers stroke the barren shrubs, where strangled
resins now will sigh, set scents afloat.

A distant rumble summons us to tryst. We cast
our chapped and withered regimens aside
for one moment of instinctual bliss. Nostrils wide,
we infuse our husk-dry spirits.   *RAIN*.   At last!

BOSQUE DEL APACHE

Between the arid foothills of the San Pascual Mountains to the east and the Chupadera Mountains rising in the west drifts the primal call of a gliding sandhill crane. Unlike the melodic twitter of songbirds, the crane's clattering clarinet voice conjures fantasies of primordial marshes.

When that voice is multiplied by 10,000 or more (the number of cranes who winter here in the Bosque del Apache National Wildlife Refuge), the resulting chorus can convince susceptible hearers that they have stepped back in time 2.5 million years, when these birds entered the fossil record. At least, visitors at each November's Festival of the Cranes claim to feel that way.

This 57,000-acre tract straddling the Rio Grande was designated a National Wildlife Refuge in 1939. At that time, observers counted only 17 of these large, heron-like birds within its confines. Since then, the numbers have grown immensely, not only for cranes but also for geese (20,000 a year), ducks, and other birds. Flocks congregate in the core of the Refuge, 12,900 acres of moist soils, where the flood plain of the river joins waters diverted by man to generate riparian forests, farmlands, and ponds that support more than 300 species of birds, as well as reptiles, fish, arthropods, amphibians, and mammals.

Bosque del Apache is Spanish for "Forest of the Apache," recalling the time when traveling Apache bands camped in stands of cottonwoods and willows along the river's edge. Among the hills that sweep away from the river, artifacts from other peoples remain: one can still see pueblo ruins of the Piro Indians or remnants of the Spaniards' El Camino Real, the Royal Road, that for 300 years guided travelers from Mexico City to Santa Fe.

LEGACY

Across a wintry backdrop filled with prophecies of snow,
a skein of sandhill cranes uncoils on the way toward rest.
Russet flickers under wings from the reflected glow
of flame-to-ember sunset banked against the west.

Earth's oldest bird, now sailing thermals over sage and sand,
once soared above savannahs that stretched to cooling seas.
Pterodactyl echoes sound from this primeval band;
wings of feather beat like leather on the buoyant breeze.

These elders of the airways flew in ages-old migration
when man was but a fledgling, and the world was wrapped in cold.
Now, humans are a factor in a delicate equation,
and—*if*—we keep the balance is a tale yet to be told.

III.

NATURE'S PUREST RAY, SHARPEST CLAW

OASIS AND FORTRESS

If water is the lifeblood of the Bosque del Apache Wildlife Refuge, then wetlands are its beating heart. Clouds of wintering cranes and flocks of flickering snow geese seek out these bottom lands for food and shelter. The Refuge has many human friends: those who band together to enlarge its lands, and those who tend fields of grain, only to share the harvest willingly with feathered migrants who arrive in autumn.

Farmers plant, tend, and then mow down grain fields row by row over the fall and winter, laying stalks in crosshatched mats upon the ground. This gives the wary snow geese a clear view all around. No tall grasses or shocks are allowed to stand to provide cover to the clever, hungry coyote or other predator who travels over land.

At dusk, thousands of birds return from daytime feeding grounds up to 50 miles away. This process of assemblage is called the "fly in." Birds of many species crowd the channels and lagoons that deter dry-land creatures who have also taken up residence in the Refuge: mule deer, coyotes, porcupines, rattlesnakes, raccoons.

∽

At night, still ponds reflect the constellations of Gemini, Orion, the Pleiades, as a cavalcade of stars slowly arcs across December skies. The glassy sheets of water serve not only as mirror but also as moat; they encircle a fortress of closely gathered birds. Sentinels listen intently for tell-tale splashes of a stealthy paw. On quiet nights like these, water amplifies every ripple, every whisper, every tune (even the vibrations of the hovering moon).

SANCTUARY

As the refuge in the desert drifts toward sleep,
a gentle segregation occurs among its guests.
Waterfowl divide by kind, as kindred keep
close to brothers, seeking sustenance and rest.
Among those clothed in feathers, quarrels cease;
all shelter in the water when day shelters in the west.

Water all around fulfills a need
for waterfowl who congregate at night.
It wards against lone hunters with four feet,
tan fur, long tail–whose yips sound out of sight.
The moat-surrounded flocks find safer sleep
than those who doze on land in dry moonlight.

Hunting Grounds

Teals, mallards, cormorants, cranes, red-winged blackbirds, swans, even gulls—the list of birds tallied so far in the unlikely oasis of the Bosque del Apache National Wildlife Refuge includes 377 species.

Prominent on the list are the birds of speed and talon: red-tailed hawks, eagles, owls, and the fierce, carnivorous roadrunner. Raptors and other birds of prey find rich pickings in the Bosque del Apache, where snakes slither and lizards skitter across exposed sandbars; mice, voles, gophers, and other small mammals burrow in banks; and minnows, bass, frogs, and salamanders abound with other aquatic creatures in the irrigated marshes and narrow riverbed.

For gentler birds, who must be vigilant to avoid sudden attack from above or swift strike at ground level, survival is a game of chance enhanced by massive numbers.

∽

Like torrents of confetti, flocks of snow geese surge in billows of flashing white bellies and flickering black wingtips. They tumble, curl, and swoop in synchronous agitation as a lone silhouette circles purposefully in upper reaches of the turquoise sky.

Cuatro

wheeling bald eagle
raises clouds of startled geese
birds rain down slowly

≈

hawk waits on tall snag
vole's darting dash through stubble
cannot outrun fate

≈

cormorants spread wings
above sunny log to dry
contemplate more dives

≈

swans leave rippled wakes
reflections jostle behind
like young disciples

Of Bird Counts and Counterfeiters

Few states surpass New Mexico in its abundance of wild birds. The state boasts more than 500 avian species with self-sustaining populations living within its borders, including aquatic birds like pelicans, gulls, herons, swans, and cormorants.

The terrain provides myriad habitats, varying from lava fields in the Valley of Fires to a large lake impounded by Elephant Butte Dam; alpine meadows in Valles Caldera (the giant, shallow bowl left by the collapse of an ancient supervolcano) to pine forests sheltering Bonito Lake. Sparkling streams water the mountain slopes above Eagle Nest, where Picuris, Taos, and Pecos tribesmen of precolonial times sought feathers of the Golden Eagle for sacred ceremonies.

✍

With the sun just rising through a gap in the Manzanos, we are out early enough to inhale hints of dampness. Beads of dew festoon a patch of prairie grass near the acequia; a shaft of sunlight transforms plumed tips into clusters of spun-glass angel hair like those of remembered childhood Christmases. The dew will not survive the thirst of the noontide sky. We stop for the moment this miracle exists. Now, no crunch of footsteps drowns out the twitters of Willow Goldfinches feeding on seedheads at water's edge.

Farther along the road, the double-note trill of the Wood Thrush. Invisible in brush lining the sangría to Mariano's hayfield, the raucous squawk of ring-necked pheasant. As usual in cool dawn or twilight hush, we hear floating, flute-like tones of mourning doves. Dawn has its own soundtrack.

Ah, but the mimids, those counterfeiters of birdsong! Yet, of the eight possible perpetrators, we know it must have been the incessant Northern Mockingbird we heard yesterday and at each awakening in the night—with notes so true we doubted the veracity of other (lovely) throats.

REPOSITORY

Songsmith, forger of the lore of birds,
you meld into one lode the borrowed veins
of a hundred more whose strains would go unheard.

Before the cock has roused himself to crow
the sleeping world's nocturnal dreams away,
you weld your silver cadences into their flow.

Mockingbird, you toil with fervid zeal,
as if enjoined to store up in the now
a hoard of melody marked with your seal,

as if you see a future fashioned wrong,
when all other voices might be stopped, and you
alone remain—our only vault of song.

Paseo de las Floridas

Acequias along this stretch of the Rio Grande engage the land in an interplay that benefits life and revitalizes this sliver of our planet. Canal seepage filtering through clay and sand recharges aquifers; saturates roots of cottonwoods, wild plums, and willows; builds habitats for birds, beavers, muskrats, and frogs. Vegetation stabilizes ditchbanks and lessens evaporation with its shade. Gravity-flow acequias wend gently south, fan into divergent streams that divide and conquer floods resulting from faraway mountain storms.

Above and below the soil, ecosystems harbor the visible and hidden. Despite misconceptions that deserts are barren, this high desert teems with life. At the ditch rider's signal in March, the waters begin to run, and the ditchbanks ready a botanical pageant, a Parade of the Flowers.

Petals like white porcelain cups belie the April bindweed's true identity as botanical ninja. May's bachelor's buttons match the blue of distant mesas. In a June dawn, white tasseled grasses catch rays of rising sun and dazzle like snow. After nighttime monsoons in July, creamy orange globemallows vie for space with wild lantanas waving ruffled purple pompoms. An August presence prompts red and orange penstemon bells to peal from breeze-blown towers. September sees spiky leaves, gold trumpets blaring, heralding green gourds prized by local artists.

But October, ah, October! Hedgerows of yellow Mexican sunflowers tower along the ditchbanks, arching under their own weight, forming floral tunnels through which a boy on a small horse can pass unscathed, if not untouched. October—when leaves turn gold and the water is turned off.

In November, russet-stained bushes and straggling amber-colored grasses begin to fade to dun. Under the drying soil and pale sun, the roots of bindweed contemplate the four short months they are given to prepare for March's return.

Bouquet Olé

Full many a flower is born to blush unseen,
And waste its sweetness on the desert air
        —Thomas Gray
        Elegy Written in a Country Churchyard

Full many a flower adorns the desert floor,
unseen by human eyes, but still its beauty glows.
Cascades of yellow Spanish Broom in summer flow,
ignoring fame the poet might bestow.

Scent is not wasted on the arid air.
Observe the hummingbird that hovers Lupine's bloom,
the flush of butterflies hoping to consume
Dune Primrose promises afloat on lush perfume.

Wildflowers do not need our elegies,
nor does their universe depend upon our seeing;
their worth is known, praise sung by lighter beings,
who taste that sweetness and discern its meaning.

IV.

SACRED LAND, SACRED WATER

Las Conchas Fire

A tree in the Santa Fe National Forest topples onto an electric power line, ignites an inferno. Fierce winds fan the conflagration; 90 minutes after it is sparked, the smear of smoke that drifts northeast over Los Alamos, 12 miles away, is visible from space. In one day, the flames race through 43,000 acres of heavily forested mountains, devouring juniper, cedar, and pine at the rate of an acre per second. The Forest Service labels the menace Las Conchas Fire.

The demon blaze sweeps north onto sacred ground of the Santa Clara Pueblo (in the native Tewa tongue, *Khá p'oo Owinga*, or Valley of the Wild Roses). This tribal homeland on the Rio Grande loses 16,000 acres in the fire, including 45 percent of its watershed.

Villagers must also flee tiny Cochiti (KOH-chĭ-tee) Pueblo, the northernmost Keres community. It lies on the west bank of the Rio Grande, near the confluence with Rio Santa Fe, which flows east through reservation lands.

Before they are sated, the ravenous flames consume more than 156,000 acres, more than any previous New Mexico forest fire. At night, the sky glows dingy red, like the gates of Hades. By day, the dull sun climbs through pallid skies scoured with talc-like grit and plumes of acrid, taupey smoke.

Novena de las Lágrimas

Nine days, and the waterways are weeping tears of ash.
Smoke curtains the Manzanos' sandstone stair.
A hundred miles away, Las Conchas still on fire.

On sludge-tainted bank, a silver flash:
a fish flaps, gasping, in thick water or dead air.
Even this far south, amid trash trapped by wire

grid across the gate, mallard ducks are mired
in greasy charcoal residue. The burn scar
on the earth will heal as decades pass,

and birds will fly again, and trees aspire
skyward. 'Til then, I say novena for you, Santa Clara,
Cochiti. I beg mercy de estas lágrimas.

SAN YSIDRO LABRADOR

It is the Blessing of the Fields at El Rancho de las Golondrinas. At the center of the procession is a litter bearing a woodcarving of San Ysidro Labrador, patron saint of acequia farmers. Many tags (Worker, Farmer) accompany his name, spelled with an I elsewhere in the world. In New Mexico, we spell it with a Y, the letter whose arms stretch toward the clouds.

Venerated as the patron saint of day laborers, peasants, and field hands (having been one himself), Ysidro is also the patron of farmers, ranchers, rural communities, and the poor. He is known also for his kindness to animals; he is patron saint of livestock and a central figure in the Blessing of the Cattle.

Parents seek San Ysidro's intercession to avoid the death of children; the drought-stricken ask his help in bringing rain. At least two New Mexico towns honor him: one on the Jemez River bears his name, the other (Corrales) claims him as its patron saint, as do numerous places in the Philippines, South and Central America, and Spain, including Seville and his native Madrid.

The legend goes that, when Ysidro Bonden's coworkers complained he was always late for work, their master visited the fields in early morning to chastise the tardy field hand. The master found the pious peon kneeling in prayer while an angel did the plowing in his stead, driving a yoke of white oxen and doing the work of three men.

One legend tells of the child who fell down a dry well, only to float to safety when Ysidro's prayers miraculously filled the well with sparkling agua. Another story says that he caused a fountain of fresh water to gush from dry earth to quench his master's thirst.

His symbols are a spade and a sheaf.

Fray Juan Chacón Blesses the New Ditch

Isadore Bonden

Blessed Isadore

Isidro Labrador

Yours are the virtues we would make our own:

love for this land, humble service to the poor,

respectful care for animals who aid our labor.

Isadore the Worker,

we beg God's favor

Isadore the Farmer,

to keep away harm

Ysidro del Madrid,

we'll do as God bids.

V.

La Comuna

Mayordomo

The white pickup with the Middle Rio Grande Conservancy District decal raises a cloud of superfine dust as it rolls toward us, but stops short on the shoulder of Orono Road. Remarkably young (he looks to be in his early twenties) for a ditch rider, the driver slides out of the truck to greet his older colleague, who leans against the MRGCD backhoe, sipping coffee and assessing the clogged culvert ten feet below.

Spring is near, and all await the word of the ditch rider telling when the water will be released. Descended from mayordomos (ditch bosses) of bygone days to oversee acequia systems, they are paid from Conservancy fees charged the users, rather than directly by the propietarios (landowners of irrigated properties) as in the old days. A few supervising private ditches in Tomé and Isleta still bear the venerable title *mayordomo*; but since the Conservancy was established in the 1920s, most locals refer to them as "ditch riders."

The duties of the mayordomo have changed little since the days of Medieval Spain: he (or she, in this equal opportunity age) must be custodian and conservationist, guardian of custom, finder of compromise, supervisor of labor, superintendent of roads. He must monitor ecosystems along the ditch; apportion water justly and impartially; and adhere to centuries-old principles of communal benefit and shared risk. He must be socially adept at settling disputes between neighbors, which is perhaps his most important job.

The mayordomo is an iconic figure in New Mexico folklore and history. Especially in the acequia societies so prevalent in the northern parts of the state, he was the most powerful person in town. He often served as *de facto* mayor, magistrate, sheriff, and deacon. Even today, in some villages, mayordomos hold the sole elected office below county level.

DITCH RIDER

Orlando José Luna can't believe his luck:
five years out of high school, and a job with decent pay.
He's known these ditchbanks all his life;
it's where he fished for bass and mastered his dirt bike.
His ditches—HIS—they've given him Tomé,
El Cerro, too! Plus usage of the truck.

An aerial map, ¡que suave! That's what God must see!
Hidden lanes form grids of numbers now,
but Abuelita beat them to it, told him their true names.
Four hundred years of Lunas, but the covenant's the same.
Orlando José Luna (in his way) makes a vow:
"Ditch rider número uno? Might as well be me."

AUXILIO

The ditch is full: 15 feet of water from bank to bank. We have seen the bottom of this secundaria when it was dry, a 7-foot stretch of edge-curled adobe shingles. Now we guess the depth of the wedge of water to be eight feet. It would wash over, were it not for the desagüe, the overflow drain leading back to the river. A fit couple on an ambling morning walk, we can just keep pace with a twig bobbing along in the current.

Did the word go out too soon? The water is supposed to be shut off tomorrow, a full six weeks earlier than usual, and farmers are forgoing their third alfalfa crop this season. Perhaps it was the unexpected downpours in the northeast (on La Bajada, the rain so heavy it washed his white diesel pickup clean), and even here in the valley, monsoon showers three days in a row.

Maybe the water will be sent downstream. Elephant Butte Reservoir holds only 10 percent of what it could contain; pecan orchards and chile fields thirst in the Mesilla Valley to the south.

Here, where the secundaria we walk every morning forms a T with what we had assumed to be another watercourse, we get an answer to our perennial question: The adjoining, still pool cannot be a supply line; it must be a drain.

From this spot on the road, we look left and see water cascading from the 4-foot-wide concrete cylinder protruding from the embankment. Muddy water spills into the turbulent flow heading east toward the Manzanos.

Looking right, we see the lagoon as it was yesterday, unmoving patches of algae, green grayed in the shade of overhanging cottonwoods. Two egrets wade the shallows, hunting bank and bog for frogs, fish, and lizards. The snowy birds flash in a dagger of sunlight piercing the leafy canopy.

Terms below paraphrased from the glossary in *Acequia Culture: Water, Land, and Community in the Southwest*. University of New Mexico Press, 1998 by José A. Rivera.

Auxilio: The custom of one ditch allowing some of its own share of stream waters to be diverted and used by a nearby ditch during periods of drought or specific emergency need.

Secundaria: A lateral trunk line between the main ditch and sangrías (trenches to individual parcels).

Desagüe: A small channel or outlet used to drain surplus waters or lead them back to the river from the last user at the "bottom" of the ditch.

QASIDA OF FAITH

That's the way it was....If there's a cup of water there, we will share it.
— Juan I. Valerio, Mayordomo, Acequia del Rio Chiquito

Monsoons come from mountain lair . . .
San Ysidro hears our prayer!
A fire burns in Santa Clara . . .
Release the gates, send water there.
At cloudless skies our farmers stare . . .
Rains will return, do not despair.
The widow's garden wilts; sun's glare . . .
Give her the portion that is fair.
Have we no water we can spare?
All must guard what's left with care.
One cup only, cisterns bare . . .
They are our neighbors; we will share.

SACAR LA ACEQUIA

Society puts an onus on New Mexicans to live within the land, rather than on it. We are constantly reminded that water is a scarce resource, and that we bear personal responsibility for its conservation. Elsewhere in this country, water is purchased as if it were a commodity. In much of New Mexico, acequia members own the conveyance systems in common, and the landowner irrigator owns the water right attached to his property. Acequia members view the systems as a community resource to which all have rights and obligations. One of those obligations is sacar la acequia (cleaning the ditch).

For at least 400 years, New Mexican communities that depend on the acequias for survival have gathered in the spring (and sometimes again in the autumn or as necessary) to clean and maintain the systems—clearing weeds and debris; repairing ditchbanks where gophers, muskrats, and beavers have dug or dammed; checking gates; replacing flumes; dredging clogged reservoirs.

La limpia, or the collective cleaning of the ditch, like many other rites of spring around the globe, is a time of community bonding. Participation on dia de la saca (cleaning day) is a hands-on experience that promotes a strong land and water ethic, inculcates a unique sense of place, and is a rite of passage for any citizen who expects to be accepted into acequia society. Working on the ditch is a public declaration that one will do one's part, but it also places an obligation on others to respond with acceptance.

Neighbors who share in bounty when water is plentiful or in deprivation when ditches run dry are expected to rally as if they were extended family when a neighbor celebrates a joy or confronts a catastrophe.

DÍA DE LA SACA

Moved in just two months ago; the subtle ultimatum:
"La limpia these two days; surely, you'll be there?"
As the second Anglo couple in this old Hispanic town,
they knew this test eventually would come;
pull shovels from the shed and tie back Swedish hair,
work until hands blister, muscles groan.

The phone rings, "This is Blanca, your neighbor from next door;
I saw you working at the ditch. Bad news . . .
Twelve-year old Yolanda was found crushed beneath her horse."
What are her chances? Helga asks. Blanca answers, "Poor."
You're making enchiladas? I'll bake bread and start a stew.
Who'll go to clean their house? Of course! What are neighbors for?

Political Currents

The two-lane highway paralleling the Belen Ditch bears on its shoulders billboards sporting moral judgments, business blandishments, political slogans, and ongoing battles between "progress" and tradition: *Widen this Road. Save our farmlands—No bridge in Tomé! ¡Tierra y Agua!*

Three simple words that carry centuries of meaning—*Tierra y Agua*/Land and Water. More than a mantra, the soul of a people. For centuries, the three strands in the rope of New Mexico politics have been historic land grants, water rights, and the Church—earth, water, and the fires of faith. The effort to institute Christian rule began as soon as Spanish missionaries arrived in 1598.

Because the number of communities soon outstripped the number of priests sent to govern them, many settlements were left to their own devices. Survival of the community was paramount, and practices that regulated the region's acequias were a natural fit to maximize a group's chances.

New Mexico has 800-900 acequias. When the region became a U.S. Territory in 1851, the convening legislature enshrined in law acequia customs and precepts that had evolved since 1598. Article I, Chapter I of the *New Mexico Territorial Laws* codified these axioms: irrigating cultivated fields took priority; all who used the ditches had to help maintain them; animals were not allowed to injure fields or contaminate the water; and the course of existing ditches could not be disturbed. Food. Community. Conservation. Law. Self-government.

Time and again, New Mexico courts have upheld the state's acequia associations' status as authentic political entities and reasserted their importance as, in Prof. Rivera's words:

> *a model institution* [that] *perpetuates cultural continuity, a sense of place, and a system of direct, participatory democracy. . .a modern-day treasure with roots in the medieval Old World and an opportunity to contribute to global diversity in the 21st Century and beyond.*

Water Democracy

Manuel Martínez has a field of beans,
as did his father before him,
and a wife whose garden blooms
with chile, corn, and pumpkin.
Manuel owns a pig; for milk, there is a goat.
In matters of the waters, Manuel has one vote.

Don Felipe Vargas has stables full of horses,
a hacienda sprawling on the hill,
a mine producing silver from richly laden ores,
and fifty labradores to till his fields.
Acequias run low, the chance of rain remote,
Don Felipe casts his single vote.

VI.

FOLKLÓRICO

La Llorona, the Weeping Woman

Angelo says he wanted to romance the lovely Gloria Delgado, but his mother forbade him, a teenager, to go to the dance, even though it was being held in the town hall. After everyone was abed, he slipped out the back window and took the ditchbank shortcut toward town. As he drew near an indistinct figure standing at the intersection of the ditches, his skin began to prickle, the air turned chill, and the ditch water glowed green. Angelo reversed his steps, the word *disobedience* buzzing inside his head.

The next day, he heard about a knifing outside the dance, sparked by jealousy over a certain girl. He says he never told his mother about his eerie encounter, nor did he ever again slip out at night.

✍

La Llorona (lah yoh-ROHN-ah), the Weeping Woman, walks the weed-choked ditchbanks in the dark hours, searching for her drowned children. She haunts arroyos draining into the Rio Pecos or Rio Santa Fe, wailing for the children she sacrificed in a vain attempt to marry a rich man. She seeks vengeance upon the carousing husband whose children she slew to spite him when he deserted her for another woman. She lurks at crossroads to steal children to replace those she murdered—or to repeat the crime.

She wanders the waterways eternally, barred from Heaven until she can answer St. Peter's question, "Woman, where are your children?"

A story to keep children away from dangerous ditchbanks? Errant husbands in line? An archetypal shrieking spirit or murderous mother reminiscent of Ireland's Banshee, Greece's Lamia and Medea, or the Aztec goddess Cihuacoatl? La Llorona is New Mexico's persistent, at least half-believed fable of betrayal, retribution, and remorse whose numerous versions always start, "Right here, right in this town, there was this woman . . ."

CROSSROADS ACROSTIC

Wail from the daggered claws of dank and brambled reeds,
Eternal mourner, sojourner robed in widow's weeds.
Entreaties pour from your writhing mouth in torrents.
Peace I cannot grant until you kneel in penitence, but
I shall sentence your betrayer to an equal punishment, for
Never has the man confessed he brought death to innocents, nor
Groaned in contrition, as **you** moan through midnight hour, or

Wept with the admission he abused those in his power. So,
On him and his arrogance be this unending curse:
May your pardon be the cup he seeks to end his endless thirst.
Ashamed, sharing half the blame, he shall roam the watercourse,
Never to catch up with you, nor leave behind remorse.

Fish and Game Department

The gurgling *g-g-g-g-g-g* call of a tom turkey chucks from a backyard pen or farmer's acreage on the other side of the acequia. I recall the four Rio Grande wild turkeys my sister pointed out in the stand of spruce and pine near her house on Eagle Creek. Hard to believe the Butterball™ she served at the holiday feast was the same species as those roaming the nearby tributary of the Rio Ruidoso.

These stream-loving birds have been a part of human culture in this, their native land, for at least 2,000 years. They supplied both food and feathers, which were highly valued by ancestral peoples for both ceremonial and practical uses. Their feathers were woven into blankets; their antics captured in ancient dances; their humorous behavior embodied in the Aztec god Tezcatlipoca.

Deer and elk, turkey and ptarmigan, pheasant and quail, rabbit and duck, fat prairie chicken and plump-breasted mourning dove: game animals and birds that fed ancestral puebloans, Hispanic colonists, and Scottish and Irish cowboys pushing cattle along the Rio Hondo when New Mexico was still a Territory. Today's inhabitants harvest them still.

The hunters vary: ranchers wanting a change from beef; farmers unwilling to give their crops over to cottontails and jackrabbits that may be tough but tasty; impoverished laborers who supplement their tables with pan-fried bass and catfish pulled from the ditch on 10-pound test line or with browned, braised dove and quail brought down with buckshot.

New Mexico has its share of vegetarian newcomers; however, people descended from old families who subsisted by using every available resource have few qualms about harvesting the finned, furred, and feathered creatures drawn to wild or man-made waterways. But they maintain the tradition of ensuring this bounty will be there for their descendants.

SILENT PARTNER

Gray-feathered clouds enshroud the early morning.
Across the tasseled grass and fading dew
drifts a wounded voice, "whoo-oo-oo-oo,"
a haunting birdsong, full of sorrow, yearning.

Mourning doves–forever mates–
I wait in vain to hear the partner's call
from splintered fence or crumbling wall,
distant willow, garden gate.

In the tongue of doves, *love* is a word much spoken,
fidelity a vow that's kept lifelong;
but for all faithful creatures, there comes a final song
when one who's left behind will cry, *Forsaken*. *Broken*.

Every Day a Feast Day

Splendid September afternoon. Lowered windows fill the car with crisp air and the aroma of green chile roasting out of doors. As I drive from the village of Isleta to the old town of Belén, I parallel La Acequia de Nuestra Señora de Belén de la Ladera, pouring her liquid smile on farms ornamenting her banks for a score of miles. On the shoulder of Tribal Road 3, a van with doors open and hand-lettered sign: *Fruit Pies and Indian Fry Bread.*

Past the rez, more roadside stands, farms, and dirt driveways with signs promising feast for man and beast: *Local Green—Roasted $20; Piñon, Fresh Crop; Butcher Pigs 4 Sale; Tomatoes, Squash, & Corn; Cow Hay—$6 Bale.* Here, raising one's own provender is an honored family value.

New Mexico is a bastion of old ways, and its foods typify its blended cultures. Corn, beans, and squash, the "Three Sisters" of the indigenous diet, married to chile the Spanish brought from Mexico, birthed a cuisine found today in barrio, suburbia, and pueblo. Acequia associations encourage members to preserve native seeds, grains, and produce. "Anasazi beans" reclaimed from ancient storehouses are now grown for local markets.

Except for red and green chile (known here as a food, not as a spice), no food so bespeaks New Mexico as the sopaipilla (SO-pah-PEE-ah), a fried dough served as a bread to sop up sauces during a meal or drizzled with mesquite honey for dessert. Even its name is a mongrel of cultures, a diminutive of the Spanish-Arabic *Xopaipa*, meaning "bread soaked in oil."

When tortilla dough is leavened and cooked, like Indian fry bread, in nearly smoking fat, it puffs dramatically into a pocket with crispy shell and chewy interior, a perfect wedding of Old World ingredients and New Mexico enchantment.

Comida Real
(Food Fit for a King)

Her fingers speak to dough; it speaks back to her hands
through spongy stretch of gluten encasing latent bubbles
warm as puppies sleeping in a slowly westering sun.

The pliant pillow yields a sigh as the heels of her hands
sink under body's weight toward the flour-dusted table,
sculpting what she yearns for as she lifts, kneads, and turns.

Released by rocking motion, weaving rhythms of her hands,
a remembered spell of guitar, fire, fandango. He was trouble
that she welcomed, when he sauntered through the room,

his eyes a sparkling challenge when he took her by her hands.
Like a sopaipilla deftly lowered into a simmering kettle,
she slipped beneath his surface, let her universe expand.

VII.

HEALING WATERS

CANINE ENCOUNTERS

Time was, neighbors became acquainted when called to labor by the mayordomo. In some places, such is still the case. In our rural setting, dogs encountered on ditchbank walks are the emissaries of introduction. Our neighbor two streets over comments that, long before he learns his neighbors' names, he knows their dogs and their cars. On our daily rounds, we say hello to:

Preso Canario **Jean Deaux**; massive head, cream and caramel coat, caramel disposition.

Rezmerelda, reservation dog found lost and starving by the Indian Health Services dentist. Happily adopted, now sleek and healthy. As we cut through the vacant field to the ditch, she watches from her shady spot.

Hyperactive, lonely **Macy**. Australian Shepherd/Border Collie, tail like black fringe; goes tummy up when scolded.

Mojo, laid-back golden Lab, strolls to the fence with **Teddy**, whose fluffy, question-mark tail fits his intelligent, inquiring eyes.

Ill-tempered **Smokey**, inhales a snarl through small, sharp teeth before the nasty bark. His protégé, **Beau**, Irish Wolfhound just past puppyhood, leans front paws on a tall fence he could clear anytime.

Quincy, friendly on leash, serious watchdog on her turf. Blue Husky eyes. Thrown from a truck as a puppy, fiercely defends those who took her in. **Tipper**, a golden mutt with a desultory bark, hands us off to Quincy and heads for the porch.

Little, three-legged **Haley**, watched over by big sister German Shepherd **Sasha**.

Sunny (for his disposition), Westminster champion *Bouvier des Flandres*, and his four look-alikes. Protective, fearless, big; great choice for this single woman whose property abuts a road no one patrols.

Gisa and **Tolle**, exquisitely trained German Shepherds walk off leash, ignore the dove faking a broken wing as they pass her nest.

Fences keep strangers out, dogs in. Steep, slippery acequias are no place for roaming canines.

But I Will Grieve for You

The sandy soil of ditchbank road, pocked
with puddles from last night's storm. Here, the herringbone
stitch where doves promenaded; there, a large dog walked,

leaving its deep print. Too big for a coyote—and why was it alone?
Where is the muddy stencil of its human's shoe?
The turbid waters of the stream flow swiftly on.

At the concrete culvert where the ditch divides in two,
the detritus of flood floats in an eddy.
Sodden soccer ball, gray grocery bags, a plastic cup–bright blue.

My disgust turns to heartbreak, knees weaken, breath unsteadies.
Half-hidden in brown foam and trash, brown fur bobs and circles:
pet, best friend, or "just a dog," abandoned, bloated body.

Covering His Tracks

They read the list of last night's guests in the ditchbank's sandy registry. The deep cleft of horseshoes; by the size of arc and dirt kicked up, traveling at a trot. Here, the childlike print of an opossum's paw, there the shallow groove left by a lizard's tail. Dove tracks fractal from road rut to weed-choked edge and back. The cocksure print of a large bird (roadrunner? pheasant?) crosses the path in an unbroken line.

⋘

The sun is high and hot, and the distance her doctor urged her to walk is farther than she wants to go. He knows from the set of her lips and the way she draws in a ragged, tentative breath (as if screwing up courage to apologize or to admit defeat) that she is getting ready to turn back.

He interrupts with a speculation about the mystery at their feet: a path five inches wide that cuts diagonally from acequia to sangría, the lateral that waters the lush field of alfalfa on their left. No pawprints, just splashes of water beside a smooth swath that looks as if some creature had used a broom to sweep away evidence of its passage. Brush borne by an industrious beaver? Cover for the telltale trail of a rambling muskrat?

He asks if she remembers a certain olde-tyme fiddle tune and begins to hum it. She smiles and joins in, then they join hands and pick up the pace of their walk. After so many years together, she easily sees through his stratagem but pretends to have been completely taken in.

Variations on Kid Ory's Tune

Oh, my darlin' do you know that old tune, Muskrat Ramble?
I hear it play inside my head when I pick up my fiddle.
Let's do-si-do your fears away, and promenade the middle.
Oh, my darlin' lean on me, your trust I would not gamble.

Oh, my sweet, I do entreat you, let us gaily amble.
As we walk, we'll freely talk, our deepest thoughts uncover.
Let me brush away your tears; we ever will be lovers.,
Oh, let us journey hand in hand; I'll shield you from the bramble.

Oh, my dear, I'll be right here, should you start to tremble.
In dread of night, I'll hold you tight and let no nightmare vex you.
In light of sun, as champion, I'll be there to protect you.
Let soul be calm; now take my arm and dance the Muskrat Ramble.

Measuring the Flow

The Spanish word *sangre* is a feminine noun meaning "blood" and the Spanish *corazón* is a masculine noun meaning "heart." Sometimes it is used in the sense of "my heart, or sweetheart."

Perpendicular to the acequia madre, trenches about two feet deep branch off to individual parcels. Earthen-walled since ancient times, concrete-lined in some of today's more affluent areas, they are called *sangrías*. For the fluent Spanish speaker, the term conjures images of blood veins or bleeding.

A surco de agua is a measurement of irrigation water. . .the amount that would flow through the hub of a Mexican cartwheel placed at the mouth of a ditch. . . roughly 51 gallons per minute.

The adult human heart pumps replenished blood from a chamber on the left side of the heart into an artery called the *aorta* for distribution throughout the body. The mouth of the aorta is just over an inch wide and accommodates a flow rate of about 1.3 gallons per minute.

❧

The doctor's numbers shocked her: pulse rate, blood pressure, molecular proportions, statistics on anxiety and depression, side effects of medication, degrees of dehydration. Thirst she had dismissed as metaphoric was proven metabolic, and every measurement the doctor took looked like an aberration.

In her case, the road to recovery would meander like a river. The couple started with walks along the ditchbanks: not far at first, but too far if she panicked. He was always there, restrained but vigilant, ready to steady her with outstretched hand or words of reassurance. As weeks rolled by, the daily regimen brought longer, stronger strolls.

Most surprising was the synergy between the daily physical activity and the other nooks and crannies of their lives—intellectual, emotional, spiritual, artistic. Obligation became acceptance became expression became delight.

High Expectations

"Are you sure you want to do this?" he said, as if
the water flowing smoothly in the bottom of the ditch
were a torrent in a gorge, and the ditchbanks soaring cliffs.

For this acrophobic wife— even at her best—
two planks laid from bank to bank posed a crucial test
(self-imposed, she would admit) in learning how to trust.

She knew he would refuse if he saw fear upon her face,
so she made him turn away. Then she closed her eyes and placed
her hands upon his back. He led the way across at a gentle pace,

then turned to offer help up the slippery incline.
What was rushing through her heart as she made the climb?
Even when she caught her breath, its fervor stayed behind.

Ephemera of Consequence

Materializing from nowhere, clouds of fluttering confetti wing about our feet and heads on this late spring morning. Surely, they are hatchlings, and not migratory adults, or we would have seen them arrive like patches of calico blown in on a shepherding wind. *Chartreuse* has too harsh a sound to describe the muted hue of their inch-wide butterfly wings, a blend of pale daffodil yellow and budding hollyhock green. Nothing showy in gossamer, bright eye spots, contrasting color, or pattern, just matte monochrome as if to say, "I'm not worth the trouble. Go find something delectable."

We meet neighbors on the path, walking the unflappable German Shepherds Gisa and Tolle. Exclamations as we pass each other, agreement on the beauty and coolness of the morning and the magic of walking through drifts of tiny Tinker Belles. They call over departing shoulders, "Enjoy them while you can. Two or three days, and they all disappear."

≪⁙

We have always done our best talking while on the move. Long drives in the country, long walks together in the mountains, in the desert, along ocean beaches, on shaded suburban streets. Something in physical movement frees the tongue as well as the spirit; something in open air dispels demons of doubt and depression. Heaven knows, the words needed to be said, the anxieties brought out into the light where, united, we could vanquish them.

How could we have known the transformation awaiting us in our ditchbank exploration?

WHY I DON'T WRITE YOU LOVE POEMS

Sometimes my words seem nearly right;
I try to net them with my pen.
When phrases struggle toward flight,
I think back to that summer, when
I gathered scores of insects: glittering
beetles, bees, et al, and the gauzy-winged.

If I should capture those brief, sweet
flights of rapture when our hearts beat
in unison of love and trust,
and pin them down like specimens
for others' eyes, would they not end,
as that collection did—in dust?

Unbridled Confidence

Ordinarily, I would not walk the ditch alone, but today calls me out with hints of scintillating clarity; and I need to feel the sun's heat on my back. Invincibility is in the air.

I greet the backhoe driver patching recent overflows; step aside for dump trucks trundling dirt along the road. I can tell their loads have come from different sources by the contrasting colors at my feet, a line where Tomé tans and Romero Ranch red oxides meet.

I stop at our turnaround on Otero Road in leaf-stirred shade beneath a gnarled cottonwood. My gaze is drawn by movement fifty yards away. Beyond the skirt of tumbleweeds clustered at a pipe fence, I see the outline of an old round-pen. At the center of the circle inscribed by rusty rails stands a wiry woman, ramrod straight, wearing jockey cap and long-sleeved shirt; tucked into her riding boots are skinny denim pants.

She pivots, and I spot the lunge line that connects her to a horse fully accoutered but riderless. The beast trots the perimeter; as I watch, it circles twice again. A young bay, brown coat gleaming, with midday sunlight streaming on black tail and mane. From beneath hot saddle leather, sweat spreads down the creature's withers in a chocolate stain.

In the trainer's hand, a whip. It does not touch the horse, but threat is there. She flicks her wrist, I hear the crack of air, and the animal reverses its direction; but its carriage is unsure, it seems to want to rear, and its gait is nervous.

I recall my equestrian sister's words, "You never need a whip. It's not a test of wills or courage. To make a horse do what you want, you first must gain its trust."

Just a Line to Say . . .

How does a spider read a slender filament's vibrations
to know a moth is caught, and where it's tangled in her web?

When streamers of snow geese fly in autumnal migration,
what wire transmits the signal to follow where they're led?

When mirth is pulled from fiddle strings by veteran musician,
how does a soul speak through the bow so hearers know what's said?

If dogs can tell by leash and horse by rein there's trouble,
and angler know from tug on line if he's hooked trout or other;

if threads of time connect our tribes around a common table
and we build bands of brotherhood by struggling together;

how can I view this lifeline you extend as wishful fable,
when you hold the other end?   I grasp it as my tether.

✄   ✄   ✄

ACKNOWLEDGMENTS

I offer my deep appreciation to José A. Rivera, Ph.D. His book, *Acequia Culture: Water, Land, and Community in the Southwest*, was a primary resource for this manuscript. Prof. Rivera not only shows his mastery of the history, science, law, politics, and acequia culture in New Mexico and other locales where he has done fieldwork (Spain, Chile, Peru, the Philippines) but also reveals an abiding passion for preserving the human values and collaborative way of life engendered by this technology wherever irrigation communities are found.

I thank him for helping ensure I had my facts straight, my translations of Spanish terms correct, and for pointing me to other artists who have been inspired by this subject.

Thanks to fellow poet and best friend Kitty Todorovich for her helpful critiques of work in progress and her proofreading of the draft manuscript, not to mention her unwavering encouragement and support for this project from its inception.

I am much obliged to poet, artist, photographer, and storyteller Georgia Santa-Maria, a fifth-generation New Mexican who grew up on the historic Anton Chico Land Grant. She has so vividly portrayed her childhood in that northern acequia community that I became half convinced I had grown up in the same neighborhood. In addition to the stories, Georgia, thanks for taking photos for this book.

My daughter, Rebecca, who lives in a tiny village bordered by three Native American reservations and the Santa Fe National Forest, has my deepest respect for her insights into women's roles in such remote communities. I also salute her for her hard work to protect precious land and water by promoting sustainable agriculture. She practices what she preaches by growing much of the organic food that goes on her family's table.

✍

Most of the poems in this work are new. A few have been revised so much from earlier work that only the title and concept remain. Some have retained enough of their original lines to merit acknowledgment of prior publication, either in a collection of my poems titled *Already There* (Mercury HeartLink, 2011), or in other publications as cited:

The Rag
>"Monsoon"

Already There: poems
>"Bouquet Olé" (as "Bouquet for Thomas Gray")
>"Sanctuary" (as "Fly-in at the Bosque del Apache")
>"Repository" (as section *III. Largo* from "Mockingbird Suite")
>"Silent Partner" (as "Love Call")

Encore: NFSPS Prize Poems 2011
>"Legacy" (second prize)

small canyons anthology 2006, a haiku compilation by the Southwest Region of the Haiku Society of America
>"Cuatro"

About the Author

Shirley Balance Blackwell is a bona fide "desert rat," born and raised in mining and ranching towns in Arizona and New Mexico; she claims the Land of Enchantment as home. She and her husband live in the high desert 20 miles outside Albuquerque.

In retirement after careers in national security, the Blackwells indulge each others' passions for poetry and music. She attends and sometimes features at poetry readings and writers' workshops; he attends and sometimes plays fiddle at bluegrass, Celtic, and folk music festivals.

Blackwell's poetry appears in numerous regional anthologies, including a New Mexico Centennial volume being published in 2013 by UNM Press. Her first full collection of poetry, *Already There*, (Mercury HeartLink, 2011) was a finalist in the 2012 New Mexico-Arizona Book Awards.

www.ingramcontent.com/pod-product-compliance
Lightning Source LLC
Chambersburg PA
CBHW022136080426
42734CB00006B/385